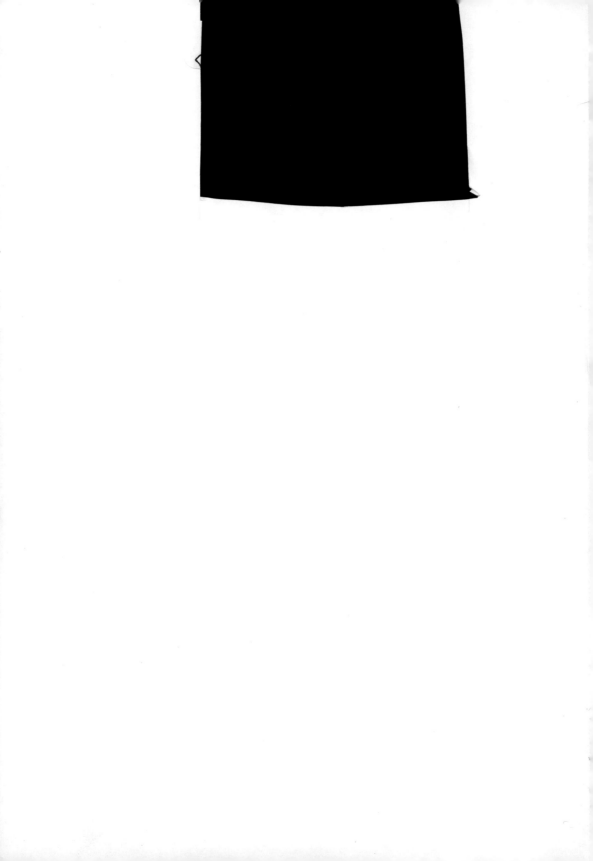

Text copyright © 1968 by Random House, Inc.
Text copyright renewed 1996 by Nancy Perkins Andrews and Random House, Inc.
Illustrations copyright © 2007 by Henry Payne.

BRIGHT AND EARLY BOOKS and colophon and RANDOM HOUSE and colophon are registered
trademarks of Random House, Inc.

www.randomhouse.com/kids

Educators and librarians, for a variety of teaching tools, visit us at
www.randomhouse.com/teachers

Library of Congress Cataloging-in-Publication Data
Perkins, Al.
The ear book / by Al Perkins ; illustrated by Henry Payne. — 1st ed.
    p.   cm.
"Originally published in different form by Random House, Inc., in 1968" — T.p. verso.
SUMMARY: Our ears hear popcorn popping, flutes tooting, hands clapping, and fingers
snapping.
ISBN 978-0-375-84251-1 (trade) — ISBN 978-0-375-94251-8 (lib. bdg.)
[1. Ear—Fiction. 2. Sound—Fiction. 3. Stories in rhyme.] I. Payne, Henry, ill. II. Title.
PZ8.3.P42Ear 2007
[E]—dc22
2006017630

Printed in the United States of America

10 9 8 7 6 5 4 3 2 1

First Edition

The EAR BOOK

by Al Perkins

illustrated by Henry Payne

A Bright and Early Book
From BEGINNER BOOKS®
A Division of Random House, Inc.

Ears

Our ears

They hear a clock.

Our ears hear water.

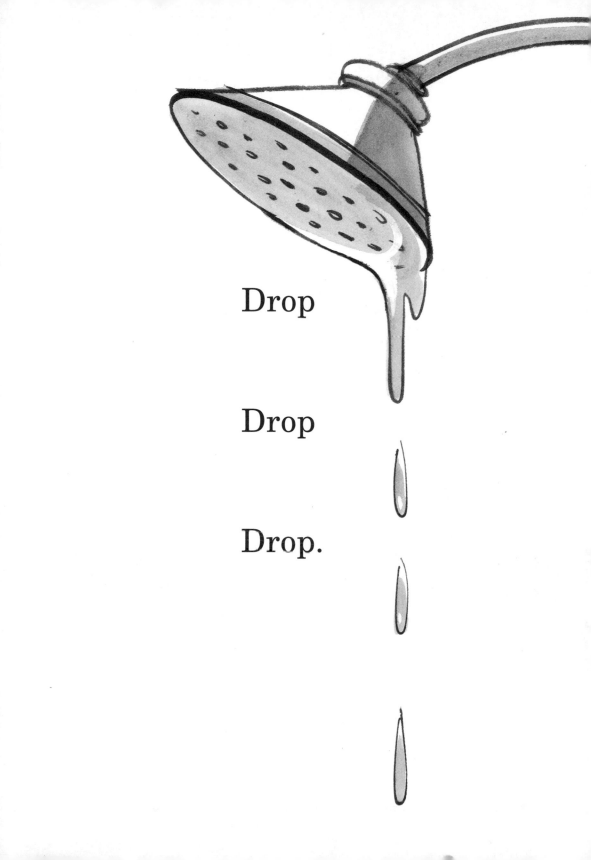

Drop

Drop

Drop.

Our ears hear popcorn.

Pop

Pop

Pop!

Ears Ears
Ears
Ears

It's good.
It's good
to hear with ears.

Toot
Toot
Toot

We hear a flute.

We hear a Ding.
We hear a Dong.

We hear a Ping.
We hear a Pong.

We hear my sister
sing a song.

We also hear
my father snore.

ZZZZZ

We hear my sister slam the door.

Boom! Boom!
Boom! Boom!
Dum! Dum! Dum!

It's good
to hear
a drummer drum . . .

and Sister blowing
bubble gum.

We hear hands clap

and fingers snap.

We hear feet
tap
tap tap
tap tap.

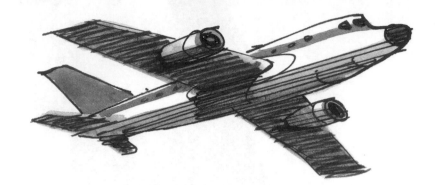

We hear a plane.
We hear a train.

It's good.
It's good
to hear the rain.

Ears. Ears. Ears!
We like our ears.
It's very good
to hear
with ears.